A BREATH OF INSPIRATION

BY

PAMELA GRANT JAMES

A Breath of Inspiration

Copyright @ 2020 Pamela Grant James
All rights reserved. No part of this book may be reprinted or reproduced or utilized in any form or by any electronic, mechanical, or other means now or hereafter invented, including photocopying and recording, or in any information storage or retrieval system, without permission in writing of the author and publisher.

ISBN: 978-1-7357337-6-0

PGJ PUBLICATIONS (Pamela Grant James)
Author contact: pamelagrantjames@icloud.com
Editor: The Sable Collective, LLC ceo@thesablecollectivellc.com

Cover Designer: Bob Ivory for Ivory Coast Media

Acknowledgements

To God, I am grateful for the gift of poetic expression, as well as His me for the we.

To God, I am grateful to wrestle with emotions and come to some understanding, or not.
And yet, I know that it is you God that never forgot.

To God, I am grateful for my family: momma, Lucretta Marie (Grant) and father, Israel Neal, My brothers: Tony (Richey), Darrell, and Israel (Grant).

To God, I am grateful for the gift of being a womb-bearer to Shannon Marie and Curtis Lee James Jr. who enabled me to sacrifice my life with joy and to know I would give up my life, if need be, without even batting an eye.

To God, I am grateful for the legacies of the Grant, Rogers, Neal, and James families who all played significant roles in the shaping of this creative work.

To God, I am grateful to the Rev. Dr. Stafford Miller who first encouraged me to put my poetry into a book about a decade ago.

To God, I am grateful for my current mentor, big brother, Bishop Charles Singletary who believes wholeheartedly in his beloved sister. He generously with compassion, faith and patience— teaches and guides, makes space, and provides opportunities for my vision and growth.

To God, I am grateful to my Spiritual Director John Algera who is directing me closer and closer to the One which allows for the unfolding of continual revelation.
To God, I am grateful for my big sister in Christ Rev. Loraine Priestly-Smith who has always stood by my side in prayer and friendship.

To God, I am grateful to Rev. Dr. Deborah Jenkins who is such an encourager who without her valued editing, empowerment and unconditional support, this book would not have been published.

To God, I am grateful to Bobby Ivory for providing the creative clothing and marketing for this soulful work.

To God, I am grateful to the NYTS community for igniting a deeper spiritual awakening of the Divine as well as allowing uninhibited expressions of my soul.

To God, I am grateful for all the churches, mosques, synagogues and other spiritual places of worship.

To God, I am grateful for my friends and especially my longest friendship with Lurlene Holder.

To God, I am grateful for my book club, and a host of many other very dear and special people as well as foes.

I say, thank you! Thank you!

For our collective has yielded,

"A Breath of Inspiration".

By Pamela Grant James

TABLE OF CONTENTS

Introduction..1
I Feel Angry...3
Sustenance...6
Secrets to Life..8

Lost..10
The Making of a Mountain..11
The Mark of the Heart...12
Control of Matter..13
A Generation Behind...14
Beyond the Eye..15
The Beat Goes On..16
The Inner Soul Comes Alive.....................................17
Sad...18
To God Be the Glory: Great Things He Has Done....20
The Face of God..21
Trust..24
What Theology Is Not..25
Where Does God Reside?..28
Dear God...30
Divine Mystery..33
Mouth to Mouth Resuscitation...................................34

Identity: Destiny Unfolds as True Love Be Told......................36

Amor..38

Still...

Not Just a Wanna Be..42

Highway Reflective...44.
Space Throughout..45
Sequences..46
What a Gift to Have a Friend..47
What's Good..49

Naked..50

Faces of Diversity..53

Grateful..54

Heads or Tales..55

In Touch..56

Pride in a Bottle...57

Forgiven..58

The Last Seed...60

Someone's Crying..61

We Remember..62

The Lamenting One..63

A Dream of Peace..66

A Simple Touch 1...67

A Simple Touch 2...69

Unsung Hero 1...71

Unsung Hero 2..**72**

INTRODUCTION

Pamela Grant James has always been in love, intrigued, inspired, imbued, and inflamed... by the Divine. This in turn has ignited her poetic expressions to bring forth emotions which capture, reflect, define, engage and move one beyond despair.

Everything is sacred, not just those things defined by society as such. So, while looking through the lens of the ordinary into the extraordinary, you will glimpse a piece of the Mosaic.

After all, "A Breath of Inspiration" together with your breaths, will unveil feelings about self, others, isms, neighbor, COVID-19 and varied crises, as well as provide a peek into the mysteries of Love.

So, be ready, to hear this unique voice from all four seasons, evoking a pondering into the known and unknown, a journey into both what is speakable and unspeakable. And at last, culminating into thought processes which give you hope for a future!

Thank you for sharing the ride!

HOPE

I Feel Angry

I feel angry at people such as those who arms are too short to reach back out!

I feel angry when I try to help you, and you are choking and chose to drown!

I feel angry that these last few months flipped upside down and I did not sniff the smelly clues, that it is going to take time to turn around and about!

I feel angry my energy is lower than normal!

I feel angry I am doing less than customary; and yet, on the other hand more than "natural"!

I feel angry about the injustices both big and seemingly small!

I feel angry that at times I sold out and did nothing at all!

I feel angry about the Covid-19 pandemic blowing right in my face, the lock down. And this disease horrifically and disproportionately is killing and affecting more blacks and browns!

I feel angry the parks are closed in inner cities. In contrast, to other spacious areas, where they get to walk in the park with air so fresh and not stale at all!

I feel angry because I am tired of fighting to be considered equal. And the discrimination in streets, stores, and workplaces. With the injustices that are even more!

I feel angry when people are blamed for a disease that kills them because they are poor, given less than healthcare, PPE, nutrition and turned away before they enter the ER door. Shouting "you are not that sick; it's just a panic attack, a cold, we don't know what you came here for!"

I feel angry when people of certain cultures who are other than black or brown are given a pass to disobey the rules, of the mayor, governor, WHO, CDC and more without considering the impact of their actions. And when confronted they have the audacity to be in an uproar!

I feel angry when people are forced to do the unimaginable and go on as if they are a blank slate!

I feel angry when people see things in just black or white!

I feel angry when there is no more love for humanity!

I feel angry at the evil some do, to greater than just a few!

I feel angry about the fear projected on people of color due to guilty consciousness' of the people in power, and with wealth!

I feel angry at all the people incarcerated for drugs, especially marijuana!

And now, it is a multibillion-dollar legal industry with exclusion, of my sisters and brothers due to incarceration because they were just trying to make a living!

I feel angry for not forgiving!

I feel angry when people act so bright and take other's light!

I feel angry that "I Can't Breathe" does not matter for black lives!

No more!

I fuel this passion to cancel the status quo of before!

Sustenance

Jesus came and did a new thing!

He broke the traditions of the Pharisees and Sadducees.

God causes change but changes not.

God sees the suffering.

A father, a mother who knows her children are thirsty and hungry.

God gives food for the body and soul.

Truth that sticks beyond the bone.

Content.

Full.

Your "cup runneth over".

Complacent,

God is not!

God is not in a box!

Not in just your world!

He resides all over the place.

Even beyond the human race.

God does not love one child more than the other.

We are all God's precious breaths.

A mother, a father with many children,

Has a special love for each and every one.

God however is both and none.

We are the apple of God's eyes,

Us daughters and sons.

Secrets to Life

Live life now,
With or without,
Frowns.

Enjoy,
The moment by moment,
Happenings and events.

Never say, "never"!
Fulfill your every endeavor.

Do not be afraid,
Of what others,
Think feel or say.

Do only what is pleasing to
God the Father,
God the Son;
God the Holy Spirit.

This is key,
To one's inner soul and peace.

It is the fulfillment of God's plan.

It is not to worry about things undone,

Or projects never begun.

It is to experience our surroundings
One
By
One.

Enjoy nature,
Honor the differences of others,
And their uniqueness in the world.

Do always what is essential.

And yet, this is not so very simple.

Love, fear God and obey the way,
Holy has set for us.

Always keep in mind,
Our life,
Is but a mist.

Urgently pursue,
The concrete,
The abstract,
And above all,
The ONE!

Lost

Like a pebble in the sea,

Like a leaf in the forest,

Like a cloud in the sky,

I sat and pondered,

Why?

Why?

Why?

Then I began to cry.

It's not fair you see!

If it's not my way.

I don't know about today.

Yet, I daydreamed until yesterday.

All I feel is insane,

Going,

Away,

Going,

Nowhere.

The Making of a Mountain

It takes a lot of sand to make a mountain.

Yes, it takes a lot of sand and years.

It takes the weathering of stones.

The accumulation of time, fine and varied minerals of every kind.

Like a student who has just begun.

Whereas, when, the teacher contributes his or her mineral,

the rock foundation is activated.

Children are pebbles full of potential.

In them Creation has just begun,

Building, building, and building.

It just does not matter how much sand is there.

Or if there is little to know.

To transform this layer…

It will take as little as a minute, hour, day, year, decade or more.

For completion of foundation to be won.

Use the obstacles,

and give it all, You got!

The Mark of the Heart

Hurt,
Comes,
In different ways.

It's most certainly,
Experienced,
Throughout,
Our suffering days.

The physical,
So much easier to bear.

Scars,
Embedded,
On our fragile hearts,

Mostly
By
People
Who,
Were
Supposed
To
Care!

Control of Matter

Like a glass,
Sometimes
Gleaming,
Then suddenly
Dull,
With the
Past,
Present,
Future,
S H A TT E RED
Into pieces,
Is the confused mind.

And yet,
A solid square at times.

Is it real…
And beholding of truth?

Influenced
By fantasy
Or non-fiction,
Wondering,
Terrifying,
Enlightening,
Expressions of many,
Like the spectrum of a glass,

Matter of control.

A Generation Behind

Children,
Children,
All the time,
Just coming in,
And out of our minds.

How did they grow?
What happened to those precious times?
What happened to God's word?
They didn't even know.
What happened to the sayings and verses like you "reap what you sow"?

How come so many who brought them here,
Who knew the Word,
And yet, did not share?

Yes, teacher! Yes, teacher! I know! I know!
It's just our selfishness that let them go!!!
It's just being into ourselves and blinded in our way.
It's going about our own business you say.

It's giving up on God and forgetting how to pray!!!

Beyond the Eye

God is so awesome!

One morning I noticed three plants of the same species.

One bud: pink, white, and yellow in color adorned only one.

It was the middle of January.

Winter!

It caught my eye.

Water filled my sight.

This reflected the Almighty alright!

Three plants, ONE Species, God the Father, God the Son and God the Holy Spirit: Trinity.

Trinity functions as One.

Today the middle one blossomed.

The Beat Goes On

I go through life,
Being trapped,
Into something,
I can no longer…bear.

I try to find the answers,
But tears are all that comes to me.

They don't know me.
If I turn the other way,
I release myself.

What is there left to do?
Despair is here!

Time does not change a thing,
Contrary to what they say,
Dust is just added.

Communication attempts lead to hell,
Finally, I blacked out...

I turn against reality.
Only to discover that it still exists.

This is how it is;
The
Beat
Goes
On....

The Inner Soul Comes Alive

The inner most being is seeking, thriving, and grasping liberty from its shields and isolated existence. It is inching--- and --- inching out but seems as though it can never make it through to its sincere purpose. Influences are upon it from every direction; piecing and shaping, the pure being with tremendous effect. It is confused as to what way to turn because all it wants to do is to be true and manifest its unique and individual personality.

Somehow, its outward environment has made it too petrifying to open up, come out, and be what he/she is struggling and straining to be. Though through it all, they remain sane and continue to survive the conflict. The overwhelming oppression is causing it to reach the limits of extreme pain and anxiety. It is hanging upon its last minute, unconscious nerve. Suddenly, it is suppressed back into safe existence and security. Yet not content.

The yearning remains to be uncovered and not manifested to itself nor others. So, it attempts to reveal its being again and then someone sees it as a reality never expressed in such depth. It touches another and finally it becomes real. No longer is it afraid to unmask its true identity.

The soul-searching journey is over. It has sought someone who understands though not perfection. It is warm blooded and very much humane. Never to be caged again. Now they have found the ultimate here on earth but thrusts to go beyond into the deep, to unravel all that can be discovered within the heart of the inner being.

Sad

Sad, you say.

Though I don't know why I feel this way.
Could it be the day?
Rainy? Cold? Monday? Or night?
Could it be such little pay?

To whom am I focused on anyway?
Could it be I would love to go out and play?
Tennis? Golf? Hiking? Swimming?
Could it be that it's just the 1st of May?

Could it be the evil that couches at the door, awaiting a crack to give way?

Could it be the things people do, say or don't say?

Well, one thing I know,
I am going to put it to death.

This minute!
Right now!!
Today!!!

DIVINE

To God Be the Glory: Great Things He Has Done

Eternity for us He has won.
He will never give up,
Until the job is done.
He gave into nothing,
Except Jesus Christ,
Not one, not two; not none.

How gracious is our Father?
How lovingly unconditional is this ONE?
That he would give up,
HIS one and only SON!

How do I repay?
How do I not let death on the cross go in vain?
Day after day... Come as it may,
"Change daily" and,
"Repent", you say.
Don't have things your way.
Don't delay!

Time is of the essence.
You can't wait.

Not another moment.
And surely,
Not a day!

The Face of God

Such a shame,
To let life pass you by,
To be blind to your surroundings,
While you just stumble without a question why.

I am okay, you're okay,
No need to change.
We nurse on milk, not steak and potatoes.

Such a shame,
Not to embrace the trees, sun, moon, clouds, rain, creatures,
events, sights and sounds,
That affect who you are.
And what the Almighty has destined for us to become!

To not consider faces,
Nor see the majestic horizon in front of us,
To be nearsighted.

We see through copycat eyes,
Day after day,
With 20/20 complacent vision.

How are we to see the face of God?

She will not reveal Herself in such finite terms.

How dare we not,
Claim all, all, all that God has prepared.

Such a shame,
Not to dream beyond what my itty, bitty mind can see.
An open invitation awaits, despite the resistant me in we.
Through me, plans of greatness she holds.
We sit back and complain,

Never the solution,
Always the scapegoat.
We stay prisoners to people, places and things.
Right under our very noses,
Shackles can be loosened,
Souls set free.

We chose to give Satan the victory.
We don't believe Christ died and rose on the Third Day.

On the left and right,
With eyes made in the image of Jesus,
How do we do not see the other?
That is indeed our sister and our brother from the same,
MOTHER!

All of God's breaths are to rise and flow freely.
Excuses abound for who we are not.
However, it is whose we are that counts.

It's life eternity,
It's heaven now,
Throughout tomorrow, tomorrow ...
While this very day bolts to an end,
The days, months...then years
The regrets,
The tears...
We whip, beat, kick ourselves and add fuel for
Satan to discourage, kill, destroy,
And mutilate!
Or is it just us we hate?

Who is waiting about to explode?

We crawl,
Reach Kindergarten
And creativity begins to stop,
And not unfold.
To never run,

Procrastinate,
Fatality of spirit awaits.

Our arrogance and pride,
lead to the failure to thrive!

We miss,
The Kairos moment!!
Trying to,
Preplan,
Prepare,
Perform in ways,
that ought not to be!!!

Trust

Does trusting in someone leave no possible doubt in mind?

Trusting relationships acknowledge each person's total being.

To take a chance is to experience something new or to accidently push rewind.

It opens the door to encounters of the soul.

Learn to trust self before extending to anyone else.

Perhaps,

Openness yields openness,

Transparency yields transparency,

Intimacy yields intimacy,

Or not.

Does the residual of trust produce reality?

What Theology Is Not

To define what theology is, is to clarify what it is not.

Theology is not orthodoxy for me, but it is correct belief for God, as one sees.

We are all God breaths. Gen 2:7 "Then the lord God formed man from the dust of the ground and breathed into his nostrils and man became a living being."

We all contain God.

Yahweh lives in us all.

So, what is correct for you may not be spot-on for me.

Nevertheless, it is part of the trinity.

Theology is not just orthopraxy. When one does what he or she does because it is the right thing. It is rather doing the things of God because we are honored, grateful and seek his face. We do what we do for others because our hearts bleeds to do so. It runs through our arteries and veins.

I am She; she is me and so is Thee.

Theology does not exist only in the Bible you see. Theology is not God in a box...

Oh! It is part of an enormous puzzle beyond trillions of pieces. As I look at this mosaic: I, we, only get a glimpse of the assortment you see.

God is so vast, so enormous; so, free.

He does not live in prisons.

She exists for our divine glory.

She is not discovered by any group in totality.

Through our finite eyes a crack reveals; incomplete.

Theology is not stagnated but ever flowing.

Reconstructing and deconstructing to those who thirst to know.

The more that unfolds the deeper and less is told.

Theology is not bound by ways,

traditions, people, time, weather, years, months or days.

Theology is not just the study of a god best for me.

Its focus is eternity.

Theology is not just the senses we know like taste, touch, sight, hearing and smell.

It is the sixth sense manifested intimate through Holy's constant communion.

Destined for revelation from this Almighty Entity.

Theology does and does not sit alone.

Theology is not contained in one mind.

Everything, everyone and all creation cry out to what God is all about!

Theology is not black or white…distinguished by race, color or creed.

Theology does not enslave, command or force.

Theology echoes and explodes!

Theology is not limited to the young or the old, uneducated or learned, weak or bold, neither farsighted nor nearsighted.

Theology is all sided.

Discovery of what theology is not,

Uncovers who God is!

Where Does God Reside?

This is how,
You know God,
Is far bigger than,
Your wildest imagination.

God does not,
Need us,
To build,
His house.
No! No! No!
We need God,
To give us,
The architectural design.

God occupies,
 "On earth,
As it is in heaven."
In a space with,
Many, many rooms,
Of impenetrable substance,
And mass,
Full of Glory,
Not the infantile energy,
Or work of a task.

No way!

However, God wants
You to know,
Her house,
Is built upon,
Her command,
Her specifications,
Nothing more,
Or nothing less,

Her will,
His way.

God qualifies,
Who is worthy,
To build,
Even one brick,
In His Kingdom.
We second guess,
But Holy,
knows what's best.

"I AM only,
I AM alone knows,
How to build,
The throne,
On heaven and earth.

I AM has a plan.
There is nothing,
To figure out,
It's all there,
And not benign.

Follow me,
Go with the flow,
Of my design.
Move with the flow,
Of what is,
… all of God's mind.

Dear God,

I am too excited about all the great things that I am doing in your name. I have never loved like this before. It is exhausting, but the sweetness of the sweat of the tears. It was so draining trying to beat all the burdens that I had, but Whew! I am so pleased that you allowed me to give them to you. It was so good when I obeyed your truth. Surrendering offered great joy. And oh, what peace.

I miss that I don't see you and that I can't hear you. But I have you embedded in my heart and soul. Nothing in all creation surpasses how you make me feel, hear, smell, taste, and see your grace.

Speaking of grace, I realize I should give it freely to others as you have given me. And your friend mercy is just as important to give liberally.

I am not sure, why, I question my existence and your great concern. I see your wonders daily. I do realize that you are so very much for me, but I must admit, I am impatient. So, please send me some more of patience.

I am working on learning more about love. This seed in my heart has flipped the switch. I have the opportunity to love those who mistreat me, talk about me, don't believe me and the list goes on and on. Thank you for the chance to grow though I suffer growing pains. Repeating the aroma that blows into me that "weeping may endure for the night", but joy comes in the morning.

Speaking of mornings, this is when I enjoy talking to you the most. I think that is part of the problem. I talk to you in prayer and song; except sadly, I don't spend the same amount of time listening to you. I need to spend more time with you; so, I can know you better and understand the secret places in your Word.

God, could you send me some more forgiveness? I seem to be running low. I recognized this when I started to accumulate a record of wrongs. Love escaped me.

Oh, God I hate to bother you some more, however, I need to have extra doses of love because this will help cover over a multitude of sins. And assist me not to get so angry or rude.

What do you say God? I know you say, "ask and it will be given". So, I claim it now! Thank you!

Your beloved,

Pamela

LOVE

Divine Mystery

What is love?

But great joy,

Which overwhelms like nothing else.

What is nature?

But flowers, trees, skies and seas.

What is the world?

But a continuous twirl.

What is the mind?

But that of experiences, wonders, mysteries of past, present and future time.

What is a baby?

But a blank slate.

What is time?

But an existing reality.

What is eternity?

But that of everlasting happiness.

What is God?

But all of these.

Mouth to Mouth Resuscitation

Oh, to breathe life into someone, how intimate, how close, and how loving. It is, as if you are saving someone's life, how heroic.

This is exactly what God does for us. The One gives breath and through the Word we are saved. Saved from the evils of this world, saved from the destruction of eternity, saved from an insatiable void.

How sweet, when God we meet, through the spoken Word.

It is the breath of life! It is a lifeguard! If only we knew and believe with all our heart, mind, soul and strength.

God gently picked up the dust like a potter fashioning clay and formed men and women from the dust of the ground. God designed the head with intelligence and emotions. The face is detailed with the eyes, nose and mouth. The lens mirrors the soul of this being. God is creating. Yahweh places the hairs ever so gently on the face to form the eyebrows. God smiles.

God styles a smile which reflects back. Both a long slender and a thick neck. Ah! God is simultaneously making the one who holds the key as well as the one who possesses the lock. Qualities are added to each one of them. God styles the woman a little more beautiful and the man a tad more brute. God says, "To you my daughter I will give wisdom. And to my son, I add more physical strength to take care of the land. To my girl I will perform the miracles to bear more breaths. Yes! This is very good."

God makes the heart of beings by examining Herself. I am moving! The heart is immediately attached to Her. A bond is created in that special Kairos moment.

Yahweh, further scrutinizes and determines. "I want them to have what I have, to see what I see, to be like me." More intricacies are formed. God identifies each and every one of these precious births. And gives them their very own fingerprint, yielding a biological document of their authenticity. I know every grove on their palms, fingertips, and every single hair on their head. I designed them for me with my will, purpose and desire.

After the entire body was complete, Yahweh thought, "I must give them life, but how? I know, I know. I will breathe into them." So, God did ever so gently. First into the nostrils, a warm moist mist, known as breath. Inhaling and exhaling deeply Herself into the rest of creation. The beings came alive: first panting, racing and then, a pace, set to a calm, synchronous, and rhythmic ease.

Identity: Destiny Unfolds as True Love Be Told

Marcus, you are my precious one. I the great I'AM determined your life begun. I the great Lord Almighty. In Gen 2:7 "Then the Lord breathed the breath of life into Marcus nostrils, and he became a living soul."

Marcus your breaths are all around us.
Your soul lives on in this earth as people talk about you, and most certainly in heaven. Your soul is eternally alive. As they witness your character, that so wonderfully resemble your faith, your very breath. Get it! It continues. I the great I'AM knew the time and the place. Yes, I chose to manifest your greatness on earth. I 'AM, the great I'AM with infinite wisdom and abundant love. While you my precious breath stay and reside in this heavenly space.

If only they knew this truth. They would all say, "Yes"! Every last one of them knowing now where you rest! Because you are in Perfect Peace, surrounded by Perfect Love, experiencing Perfect Joy, in the most Perfect Way, with ME! You would never trade places with any one of them.

They want to know why? They cry because they don't see that perfect line in the sky. They don't understand that you are mine. That I the great I'AM formed you out of the dust of the ground. That I determined this destiny found. Yes, destiny unfolds as pure love is told. Yes, my precious pure Love.
Only very, very few will fathom a Love like this. One in which I take my beautiful love back home with Me.

Remember! It is what could be all your destinies. From the very breath that gave your life. See with me there is no beginning or end. I formed you. I created you. It was my will. Still you live on eternally. Your gifts, your talents, your words, your example, stay here and continue up there.
I Am Being, Spirit and Pure Love. Let nothing less than the love I give, occupy your heart. Nothing! Don't let the enemy confuse you. Everything, everything whether you understand it or not, is allowed by me. I allowed this, and yet, it was another's choice to take his life. Though I am pleased Marcus is with me as well as others can now see the impact of a life at only twenty-two. Though some might say his life was too few.

Stop! Look! Turn around!

See the impact that this precious life made for Me.

See the glory of a destiny unfold.

See the lives affected by my very son. Who is part of the One!

See what his life speaks.

See what you must do.

See to it that you waste no time.

I will not, cannot, tell you when, your life will be through. But be ready, when I inhale, my precious breathes, back to Me. Divine was my purpose, in Marcus you see. Divine was My purpose when I called him back to be free!

Amor

Days gone by.

As quick as the wind goes through the trees.

Faces change,

Like the mountains upon the seas.

Personality differs,

As day from night.

Memories hidden on the surface,

Of the mind.

Love varies,

Like the colors of a peacock.

If Amor be true,

Then

It

Is

A

Permanent

Lock.

PEACE

Still

Stillness is a skill.

Which is attempted to be taught even at infancy: then as a toddler. And later when we go to school.

And yet, everything is about being busy,
dance classes, piano lessons, sports, plays, homework, schedules, play dates, parties...

How, then, do we undo years of embedded activity, with knowledge, occupying every second, minute, hour, day, week, month and year?

Is this the sign of a worthy person, a productive person, a talented person, or a skillful person?

How are we to undo the rush to a hush?

Where do we begin?

By trying to sit still!

This is such a hard job!

Who would have ever thought that being still is demanding work, but it is! We run, run, run, so to do contrary is so, hard, difficult, different, and counterintuitive.

As you sit still,
you see things,
you've taken for granted.

Like the petals from a cherry blossom tree,
that flows down like snow from the sky,
softly, gently, effortlessly, gliding down to earth.

The birds want to show you their wonderful majesty by moving so eloquently through the air, in front of your lens, singing as if a long-lost friend has arrived. Ah! Their colors: orange, black, red and blue... so many of different hues.

The leaves use the wind to speak to you, as it sways from left to right. I can see how it applauds me.
Then when my eyes are closed,
I can taste the wind both hungry and thirsty.
Feeling it, touch me, ever so lightly.

The neighboring trees, hop up and down, as if jumping like a child with a tantrum, screaming, look at me, look at me, look at me!

This is a small piece of the wonder encountered,

While sitting still,

In a sanctuary.

Not Just a Wanna Be

One day I sat down to the silence.

But there are always sounds...

A humming,

A crackling,

A ticking,

A blowing,

Or small voices in your head.

I wondered, "what I was doing?"

Was I a disciple of Jesus?

Or just

"A Wanna Be"?

Did I "Wanna Be" a Christian?

But not willing to live the life of sacrifice?

Why was it so hard?

Why was there so much strife?

Well, "Satan" you say.

Or is this just an easy way out?

Or was it just my evil desires and flesh wanting to go around and about?

Surely, this would not do.

I had to study it out!

How could I change so much hurt, pain and shame?

It was like being torn in two with no army left to do.

"I have to get out right now," I say.

I have to get out

And pray, pray, pray, pray each and every day.

I have to get out and fight for God until the last day.

Off my face I will go, pushing, pulling and planting so.

No! I will not be just a "Wanna Be".

But…to be like Jesus Christ,

I will fight mold, imitate,

day and night…

To see in me.

Highway Reflective

I saw flashing lights, blue, red, so many.
I wondered, I wondered, what happened?
Who might be hurt? I thought of You and called upon your Name. Whom I am sure was already at the scene. I felt better knowing you were there. I went a little further and another accident. I knew you were here too.

I called out loud and prayed on their behalf anyway. You are there and right here. I am you and you are me. It was mind boggling.

This oneness I felt.

Separate, but part of You. At least made in the image of You.
With a part that's dwelling in me too.
Survival because of you.
And with Your ever-present residence in me.

You rest and lay your precious heart in thee.
Your Presence is incredible.
Sweetly overwhelming, it causes me to pause.

Selah!

To stop rushing all about.
Pressing my ears on your mouth.
I listen for your whisper, showered by your love.
I began to weep and wail.
Wail and weep.
It is so very surreal.
This ecstasy and fear braided together.

Space Throughout

In the
total blackness
of the night,

I peered through my window.
Thinking about the mysteries of life.
There appeared a brilliant full moon,
Laid perfectly round,
And shined bright in the sky.

Wow!
How?

It dawned on my soul,
The Almighty's,
Beauties and peace,
Are far beyond light,
And truths untold.

God's greatness is mirrored in many gone before,
And abounding more.

Staring into this expanse,
A wave of peace,
Grabbed me and hugged me tight.
Even though this has been decades ago,

That night, I will forever know.

Sequences

The rain fell upon the windowpane,

Drop,

By

Drop,

Yet, with speed.

Life seems to be going slow.

But is moving faster than one can know.

Patience is a virtue.

If we sit back and wait,

Time goes on and on,

Day after day,

A pause, a break, a missed step or two.

Whew!

So, it seems,

Then continues…through,

Over here, over there.

It just passed right by you!

What a Gift to Have a Friend

What a jewel, some will never know.

But Ah!

If you do,

So very, very, very, blessed are you.

One who knows what to say.

One whose there for the bad and good days.

One who knows before you get it out.

One who knows what you are thinking about.

One who is excited about the things you are excited about.

…concerned about

…outraged about.

They are:

Willing to go the extra mile.

Willing to give a smile.

Willing to challenge when you're wrong.

Willing to be strong.

Willing to do what is best.

Willing to endure the hard-won test.

Willing to agree to disagree.

Willing to know it is you and me as well as we.

Willing to let you be free.

Willing to unveil the mask.

Willing to join the task.

Willing to persevere until the joys outweighs the woes.

This is friendship,

 As it unfolds.

What's Good

Can anything good come out of Paterson?

This not so outwardly beautiful city.

As my mom, would say,

"There is always,

 Some good,

That comes,

Out of bad."

Naked

I don't really mind if you see me, but what I fear is what you think of me when you see me.

I am afraid that your perception would be shocking.

I can't believe it! You have all that baggage, all those thoughts which flow inside and outside of you.

How could you? I repeat over and over in my head, how could I not? I echo over and over in my head.

This is who I am.

Not the picture you conjured up in your mind.

Not the enormous canvas you painted without giving who I am any time.

This is the paint you covered me with and not the bareness of my soul.

It is the story you created: not the truth I gave you so bold.

So, don't be disappointed. I AM not.

It is how I made you with every blemish and every spot.

I AM the painter.

You were created in my mind.

You can't imagine it but all that so-called abstract splashes of paint and imperfect shapes, I purposely fashioned for the appointed time.

Please stop putting your head down, look up and remove all that I didn't initially approve.

All that others placed on you and even those you barely knew.

I love to see you without the covering of your soul.

I see Myself and I AM well pleased.

GRACE

Faces of Diversity

Deep within the faces,
Glares,
A common denominator.

We all need God above all else you see.
We will never last without the ONE both now,
And for all eternity.
We will never know our child set free.
We will never love unconditionally.

We avoid the other by saying "hi" and "bye."

Allowing Satan to divide us through his lies.

Then we look and wonder, "What's wrong?"
While we sing an all too familiar song.

"I don't know what this world is coming to!"
"I just don't know why we can't just get along."
Not recognizing, it has to do with me and you.

Wake up! Wake up! Wake up!

Stop passing the buck!

It's just not going to happen,

By chance or by luck!

Grateful

G: Giving always freely.

R: Righteous no matter what.

A: Appreciative of God's discipline.

T: Totally soul out for Christ.

E: Every moment of your life committed to God.

F: Full of joy!

U: Understanding of your purpose as a disciple.

L: Loving Abba and Loving God's Kingdom.

To God, I am grateful for all He has done.

To God, I am grateful He gave His one and only Son.

To God, I am grateful for the joy I have received.

To God, I am grateful to wholeheartedly believe.

To God, I am grateful for the Kingdom which causes the evil one to flee.

To God, I am grateful for those who stood by my side and the truth they did not hide.

To God, I am grateful for another opportunity to live the life of a disciple.

Heads or Tales!

It finally came through,

As I waited in vain.

I wondered.

What it was like?

And fantasied it to be,

Like pure ecstasy,

But it had the most painful pain of all.

A hurt like only the heart could explain.

Then it had the greatest feeling of all,

A sensation of being united.

And something which could conquer all!

In Touch

In this world of many decisions,

What can a person do?

How do they know which way to turn?

The way is through God.

Though both self and others may prove helpful.

Always in life,

Decisions need to be made,

Mind boggling,

Confusing,

Depressing,

Exhausting,

Or with ease.

And yet,

The choice remains,

To do,

As you please!

Pride in a Bottle

To swallow pride and love your enemy is a very good ideal.

Easy to say,

Hard to obey,

Though every time I try,

I am stepped on,

OUCH!

Rewind,

Play,

Stop,

Play,

Rewind.

Is the only good that is birthed.

If you just feel good about yourself,

I wonder,

Is,

It,

Worth It?

Forgiven

In spite of,

My imperfections,

My faults,

My humanity,

The One is so great!

You,

Made me,

Saved me,

Gave me,

Your Son to set the record straight.

Daily the Sun signals new beginnings.

Light in a dark place.

Whenever you see the Son,

New life has begun.

Every time I see the sun/Son,

It is as if I never seen it before.

I am mesmerized, captivated and drawn to its magnificence.

No matter the climate of yesterday,

Cold or hot, rain or snow, good or bad, war or peace,

joyous or sad, plenty or drought.

The Sun rises and sets.

The Son takes our sins and sets them within.

This is what life to the full is all about!

No need to beat yourself up,

No need to fret,

No need to question the love of God,

His Son,

We just get.

Never will there be or has there been for me,

One who pays my…

Undeserving,

Undeniable,

Unbelievable,

Un-relinquishing debt!

The Last Seed

There was a bunch of flowers on the ground.

However, I singled one as the best around.

I watched it grow.

The others die.

Yet, why was this the best?

And given more care than the

rest?

I centered around it and myself.

Poof it was gone!

The others had been blocked out.

It Stood.

All alone.

Someone's Crying

Someone's crying,

Help me now.

Someone's crying,

Not

To

Be

Let

Down.

Someone's crying for a change.

Someone's crying for their life to be rearranged.

Someone's crying for help.

And say, "There has to be a better way"!

We Remember

We remember, how God created us for God's use.

We remember, we are all birthed by the Almighty Creator.

We remember, God breathed us into existence.

We remember, God loves God's children more than any other.

We remember, the "Good News" Gospel of Jesus Christ.

We remember that intimacy with God is life to the fullest.

We remember that it is to eternity we aspire.

We remember, those who have gone before us.

We remember, that from dust we were formed and to dust we return.

We remember, less we forget!

The Lamenting One

O Creator, Redeemer, and Sustainer,

I opened my heart wide to your tenderness, mercy and grace,

Which can fill every crevice, crack, hole and space.

Right now, this pump of life is ripped open,

Blood gushes out and makes me faint.

At the edge, wishing for it to stop!

I try to remember your promises of good and not harm.

Hurting children, immigrants, faithful and the poor in spirit ones, situations are well beyond comprehension.

What can I say?

What can I say?

What can I say is going on?

Why such pain,

So many tears,

So much of life that people can't bear!

Too many soldiers are no longer,

Relief came at the end of the line,

They took their lives one at a time.

Leaving more pain, hurt, anger and grief trailing miles and miles behind.

Yes, this is earth, I understand and not the prefect land.

I beg, plea, grovel, knees worn,

And heart torn.

Mind almost completely blown for a salve, to mend the Deafening sounds,

This long dreary abyss.

Questions on top of questions with no answer in sight.

Please, please, please…God make this right!

God most high.

I believe!

I trust!

I must!

I need your Presence.

Just in case… I want you to know.

Omniscient God.

The hurts never healed,

Just blown, over with layers of dirt.

As the wind revealed,

Blatant, roughness, cruelty and hatred.

I know, you know,

And too wonder, what in the world?

So again, I bleed continuing to be in great

Need.

Of the omnipotent and omnipresent One.

Come Holy Spirit come,

Come lamb of God,

Come Father, Mother come,

In a whisper or a shout!

Straining to see the rainbow,

Here I will stand in some doubt,

Surrendering to YOU.

What life is all about?

A Dream of Peace

Stars seem so far away,

Lost among the skies,

On and on for countless days.

Arm stretched long,

Leaning, and straining,

Over the windowpane.

Untouchable,

Not felt,

But held in time.

You stare,

Can't blink,

Far beyond your mind.

Drifting,

Drifting,

into a world,

Beyond humankind.

A Simple Touch 1

The power of a hand on the shoulder.

The power of an eye.

The power of a smile by a stranger or passerby.

The power of a kind and sincere word.

A thank you.

A kind gesture.

The peace of a debate when one concurs,

And doesn't try to test you.

When you pump at the beat of another's heart,

They feel very special,

Set apart.

The glory of a look, in another's eye.

That doesn't try to question why,

Make judgements or give a disgusting sigh.

When truth is better than a lie.

When liberty is given, to all I possess, own and buy.

When you reach out your hand,

Again, and again.

Since with God,

It is as plentiful,

As the ocean sand.

When you give,

To the beggar,

More than a dime.

And inquire about his lifetime,

By extending love in action Bible lines.

A Simple Touch 2

A woman touched the hem of Jesus's garment.

So, He inquired, "who touched me?"

Why?

A piece of Him was gone.

But inside the woman born.

When the gestures you display say,

"No matter what!"

Just like Jesus,

I love you anyway.

When you sit by their side,

Without ever a word,

And still they're sure they have been heard.

When you share a picture without words or sight,

And it hugs one's spirit just so very tight.

When you've led someone into the light,

Never giving up the fight.

A simple touch,

Don't dare to flee,

Allow it, allow it, allow it,

To forever embrace your soul, ever so deeply.

Unsung Hero 1

I need not be recognized or given praise.

The magnetism of the Holy Spirit guides whatever is raised.

An ordinary gal in a sense,

And yet, extraordinary,

As every one of us are!

Created from the,

One God.

Uniquely, distinctive as daughters and sons.

Sharing together the ultimate omnipotent thread.

Thinking we are masters of the world.

Until,

A Titanic,

A Pandemic (COVID-19),

Or A Tsunami…

Then, we see.

Life is not just about me.

But the all-encompassing **we**.

Unsung Hero 2

Not to live in the mists of things only just begun.
Not to allow others who look like us,
To think it's hopeless, useless, futile or
Things may never be won.

We are all unsung heroes.

We do what we do,
Not in isolation,
But in community.

We beat the paths…
already trodden,
Walk roads less traveled.

Against all odds,
Believe,
They,
Did,
Do,
And will continue.

To make a difference,
For the betterment of humanity.
Live out our compassion,
Without any thought of reward.

Except to lift another who is down,
Help the lost to be found.

Take a risk to save, if only just one.
Who knows the domino effect that will be done?
Opens their eyes to surroundings,
Ears attuned to the sounds of the cries,
With hearts that bleed, as to why?

Nostrils,
Attentive,
To the smells of a soul's decay,
Certain to another way!

One who dares to care,
With scars laid bare,

Deals with fire,
And a spirit,
Not
For
Hire!

www.ingramcontent.com/pod-product-compliance
Lightning Source LLC
Chambersburg PA
CBHW051702090426
42736CB00013B/2501